THE SECRET OF HEAVEN'S POWER THROUGH THE MIRACLE OF

LAYING ON OF HANDS

KEYS TO HEALING, SPECIAL ADVANTAGES, SPIRITUAL GIFTS, HOLY SPIRIT INFILLING, AUTHORITY, & IMPARTATION

DAVE WILLIAMS, D. MIN, D.D.

Award-winning, Best-selling Author

THE SECRET OF HEAVEN'S POWER THROUGH THE MIRACLE OF
LAYING ON OF HANDS

Keys to Healing, Special Advantages,
Spiritual Gifts, Holy Spirit Infilling,
Authority, & Impartation

by Dave Williams, D. Min, DD

CONTENTS

CHAPTER 1

THE MINISTRY OF LAYING ON OF HANDS

In this little book we are going to examine a Biblical subject which has, in some cases, been ignored, and in other cases, been carried to a drastic extreme. Yet the laying on of hands is a foundational doctrine of the Lord Jesus Christ, and properly understood will bring astonishing blessings to believers who practice it.

Countless numbers of individuals and churches regard this doctrine as inconsequential; something peripheral; "take it or leave it." Others look upon it with suspicion and confusion. Still others revere it as a mystical "cure-all." But what does our Great Text book—the Bible—teach us concerning the laying on of hands?

Hebrews 6:1-2
Therefore leaving the principles of the doctrine of Christ, let us go on unto perfection; not laying again the foundation of repentance from dead works, and of faith toward God.

Of the doctrine of baptisms, and of laying on of hands, and of resurrection of the dead, and of eternal judgment."

These Hebrew Christians were failing to mature in the faith (See Hebrews 5:12-14). The writer was encouraging and exhorting these believers to go on and get past the elementary stages of the Christian faith and move toward spiritual maturity. He then listed six elementary components of the doctrine of Christ:

1. Repentance from dead works
2. Faith toward God
3. The doctrine of baptisms
4. Laying on of hands
5. Resurrection of the dead
6. Eternal judgment

Now look at these six doctrines carefully. Don't most Christians still believe in repentance? Of course, they do! Unless a person repents, he cannot be saved.[1] Don't most Christians still believe in having faith toward God? Certainly! We are saved by grace through faith.[2] What about the doctrine of baptisms? (Notice it's plural) We still believe in:

1. Baptism into the body of Christ by the Holy Spirit at the new birth. (I Cor. 12:13).
2. Baptism in water after the new birth (Acts 2:38, 8:38-39), and
3. The baptism in the Holy Spirit by Jesus Christ, subsequent to salvation (Matt. 3:11, Acts 1:5, 2:4).

---

1   Luke 13:3-5, Acts 3:19, Revelation 2:16
2   Romans 3:25, Ephesians 2:5, 8

There would be no argument there, especially among full-gospel people. We still believe in the doctrine of baptisms.

Let's go on. What about resurrection of the dead? We better believe correctly about this subject. Paul told Timothy that Hymenaeus and Philetus "erred concerning the truth", and their error was specifically related to the resurrection of the dead. In essence Paul told Timothy that these men were teaching a spiritually cancerous doctrine (II Timothy 2:16-19). They were teaching falsely concerning the resurrection of the dead and, as a result, "overthrew the faith of some."

What about eternal judgment? Well, Bible believing people still adhere to the doctrine of eternal judgment.[3] 3 Usually, it's the false cults that teach "heaven for our crowd and annihilation for all others." "There's no hell," they boldly profess. They've erred concerning this foundational doctrine of Christ.

For the most part, however, genuine Bible believers still adhere to the foundational doctrines concerning repentance, faith, baptisms, resurrection, and judgment. But what about this other doctrine tucked neatly in the center of the list? What about the doctrine of the laying on of hands?

SOME DON'T PRACTICE LAYING ON OF HANDS AT ALL

Yes, it's true. Hebrews 6:12 teaches us the doctrine of the laying on of hands is an essential element in the basic fundamental doctrine of Christ.

---

3   Daniel 12:2, Revelation 20:11-15

That being the case, why do some churches not practice it? Why do some professing Christians not believe in it? Are they afraid it may develop into fanaticism? Whatever the reason, departing from the doctrine of Christ in any area is a serious offense, and God will not stay in a church which does not abide in the foundational truths of Christ's doctrine.

II John 1:9
Whosoever transgresseth, and abideth not in the doctrine of Christ, hath not God. He that abideth in the doctrine of Christ, he hath both the Father and the Son.

SOME DO PRACTICE THE LAYING ON OF HANDS

Some churches do practice the laying on of hands. But it has become such a ritualistic formality that nothing ever happens. When I was "confirmed" as a young boy, the robed pastor of our church laid hands on me. Nothing happened, nothing at all. It was just a form, a meaningless ritual.

Now if you are a Pentecostal, you are probably saying "Amen, Brother Dave. Meaningless rituals might go on in other denominations, but never in ours." Now wait a minute. I have something to say to you!

Some Pentecostal churches have practiced the laying on of hands in such an indiscriminate fashion that it has become more of a cold ritual there also! Every altar call, every Sunday, people walk around laying hands on anybody and everybody for any and every reason.

I used to dread altar calls in my earlier Christian years. We'd all go forward (the same crowd every week) and this hollering deacon would come around and gently whack everybody on the head as he bellowed out some sort of a prayer over them. I'm sure he meant well, but the ministry of the laying on of hands lost its true meaning and value by this indiscriminate practice and unscriptural exercise.

WHAT IS "THE LAYING ON OF HANDS?"

The laying on of hands, by definition, is an action in which one person of faith places his hands upon another person with the aim of transmitting, conveying, or imparting something of great spiritual value.

In the Old Testament, this practice was used to symbolically transfer sins. The people would place their hands on the priest, thus signifying the transfer of their sins to the priest. The priest would then lay his hands upon the head of a bull, signifying the transfer of all sins into that animal. The animal would then be slain as a sacrifice to make atonement.

In the New Testament, Jesus became both the priest and the sacrifice. Our sins really were imputed to His body while He hung on the cross.[4] Somehow, supernaturally, all of our sins were sent back into time and place upon Jesus, and all of His righteousness was sent forward into time and placed upon us. It happened miraculously when we truly repented of our sins, and expressed faith in Jesus Christ.

---

4 2 Peter 2:24

II Corinthians 5:17-21

[17] Therefore if any man be in Christ, he is a new creature: old things are passed away; behold, all things are become new.

[18] And all things are of God, who hath reconciled us to himself by Jesus Christ, and hath given to us the ministry of reconciliation;

[19] To wit, that God was in Christ, reconciling the world unto himself, not imputing their trespasses unto them; and hath committed unto us the word of reconciliation.

[20] Now then we are ambassadors for Christ, as though God did beseech you by us: we pray you in Christ's stead, be ye reconciled to God.

[21] For he hath made him to be sin for us, who knew no sin; that we might be made the righteousness of God in him.

Galatians 3:13

[13] Christ hath redeemed us from the curse of the law, being made a curse for us: for it is written, Cursed is every one that hangeth on a tree:

[14] That the blessing of Abraham might come on the Gentiles through Jesus Christ; that we might receive the promise of the Spirit through faith.

Ephesians 2:8-9

[8] For by grace are ye saved through faith; and that not of yourselves: it is the gift of God:

[9] Not of works, lest any man should boast.

Philippians 3:9
And be found in him, not having mine own
righteousness, which is of the law, but that which
is through the faith of Christ, the righteousness
which is of God by faith:

But what is the purpose for this practice of laying on of
hands today? What is the proper application and exercise
of this doctrine in the church today? Let's find out.

CHAPTER

THE IMPARTATION OF BLESSINGS

Let us now look at the Bible purposes of the laying on of hands.

TO IMPART BLESSINGS

We find in both the Old and New Testaments the practice of laying on of hands for the impartation of blessings. Read Genesis 48 for an example of this.

> **Genesis 48:14**
> And Israel stretched out his right hand, and laid it upon Ephraim's head, who was the younger, and his left hand upon Manasseh's head, guiding his hands wittingly; for Manasseh was the firstborn.

> **Genesis 48:20**
> And he blessed them that day, saying, In thee shall Israel bless, saying, God make thee as Ephraim and as Manasseh: and he set Ephraim before Manasseh.

Jacob (Israel) laid his hands upon Joseph's sons, Ephraim and Manasseh, and BLESSED them, and prophesied over them. This was done in faith. If there was no faith, there would have been no impartation.

Hebrews 11:21
BY FAITH Jacob, when he was a dying, blessed both the sons of Joseph; and worshipped, leaning upon the top of his staff.

BENEFITS AND ADVANTAGES IN LIFE

What exactly does it mean to have a blessing imparted unto you? In the Hebrew language, it means a "benefit" or "advantage," which may not be visible to the physical eye, but will become obvious in some way or another.

The first time I ever had hands laid upon me. I received a special benefit. Prior to the laying on of hands, I could barely remember where I parked my car half the time, but afterward found that I could remember things much better, especially Scripture. I had a special advantage imparted unto me. People actually thought I had received a "photographic memory." Of course, I did not, but I did somehow receive an unusual new ability to remember things more clearly than ever before.

I remember having fellowship with a brother who belonged to a particular church, one that did not believe in the laying on of hands. Consequently, my friend had never experienced this. Well, somehow, I could always remember where the right Scriptures were when we discussed the Bible. He had been a Christian for several years and I had been saved for less than a year. He would get so frustrated because, as intelligent as he was, he often had difficulty remembering where certain Scriptures were. Then I'd tell him where to look, and sure enough, he found them

Now, I didn't flaunt this special advantage. It's just something I had received freely from God through the laying on of hands.

I believe that's why mothers brought their children to Jesus, desiring Him to lay His hands on them. These parents wanted their children to have a special advantage (blessing) in life.

> **Matthew 19:13-15 NLT**
> [13] One day some parents brought their children to Jesus so he could lay his hands on them and pray for them. But the disciples scolded the parents for bothering him.
>
> [14] But Jesus said, "Let the children come to me. Don't stop them! For the Kingdom of Heaven belongs to those who are like these children." [15] And he placed his hands on their heads and blessed them before he left.
>
> **Mark 10:16**
> And He took them up in His arms, put His hands upon them, and blessed them.

Do you know what this means when it says Jesus blessed them? It means, through the laying on of hands, Jesus invoked a blessing (an advantage; a benefit) upon those youngsters that would cause them to succeed in every area of life! Now that's a precious gift.

Parents, do you want your children to have a special advantage in life? Do you want your children to have a blessing that will cause them to succeed in life? Of course, you do. Then let me ask you this question. Have you had your children dedicated to the Lord, where the elders of the church laid hands on them, asking God to impart a blessing, a benefit, and an advantage unto these little ones?

We have taken this practice of child dedication so lightly, forgetting the real reason we lay hands on the children and dedicate them to Jesus. Child dedication is a solemn time of not only dedicating these precious ones to Jesus, but a time of the laying on of hands with the intent of imparting blessings into these cherished little lives.

What an honor, to be a Christian parent with the privilege of dedicating your children to the Lord, and having a unique blessing invoked upon the. This is really one of the primary objectives of the laying on of hands: to impart blessings!

There are more benefits to the practice of laying on of hands. Next we'll see how you can receive through this supernatural practice.

CHAPTER

THE IMPARTATION OF AUTHORITY

Now we come to the second purpose for the practice of laying on of hands.

TO IMPART OR TRANSMIT AUTHORITY

Moses was told by God to lay hands upon Joshua, his assistant, in order to impart some of Moses honor (authority) unto him (Numbers 27:18-20).

> **Numbers 27.22-23**
> "And Moses did as the Lord commanded him: and he took Joshua, and set him before Eleazar the priest, and before all the congregation: And he laid his hands upon him, and gave him a charge, as the Lord commanded by the hand of Moses."

We are told more in Deuteronomy 34:

> **Deuteronomy 34:9**
> "And Joshua the son of Nun was full of the spirit of wisdom; for Moses had laid his hands upon him: and the children of Israel hearkened unto him, and did as the Lord commanded Moses."

Notice through the laying on of hands, Joshua received authority and special wisdom. As a result, the people respected Joshua greatly because, though invisible, they recognized an impartation of leadership authority upon him. This occurred through the laying on of Moses' hands.

In another case, Elisha, the prophet, laid his hands upon King Joash to impart divine wisdom and ability for successfully leading God's people.[5] Wouldn't it be wonderful if every elected and appointed official, before accepting their official positions, called for the men of God to lay hands upon them in order to impart special wisdom and ability to do their jobs effectively? If that would happen, in a matter of just a few months or less, this nation would be out of debt and would be honored and revered once again as the greatest and strongest nation on the planet! The wicked would be driven out (I Kings 22:46), the lawless would be ashamed, the rebels would come under authority, abortions would cease, sex trafficking would haul, the prison systems would shrink, prosperity would flow, and we would get a foretaste of what it's going to be like during the Millennial Reign of Jesus Christ. Hallelujah!

The impartation of divine authority is released through the ministry of the laying on of hands.

LAY MINISTERS ORDAINED BY LAYING ON OF HANDS

The truly New Testament type church is made up of

---

5   2 Kings 13

a staff of both lay and paid ministers. When the load became too heavy for the apostles, they ordained lay ministers to help.

Acts 6:5-8

...and they chose Stephen, a man full of faith and of the Holy Ghost, and Philip, and Prochorus, and Nicanor, and Timon, and Parmenas, and Nicolas a proselyte of Antioch: Whom they set before the apostles: and when they had prayed, the LAID THEIR HANDS ON THEM. And the word of God increased; and the number of the disciples multiplied in Jerusalem greatly; and a great company of the priests were obedient to the faith. And Stephen, full of faith and power, did great wonders and miracles among the people.

Notice the official method of imparting authority: the laying on of hands.

MISSIONARIES COMMISSIONED

Acts 13:1-4

Now there were in the church that was at Antioch certain prophets and teachers; as Barnabas, and Simeon that was called Niger, and Lucius of Cyrene, and Manaen, which had been brought up with Herod the tetrarch, and Saul. As they ministered to the Lord, and fasted, the Holy Ghost said, Separate me Barnabas and Saul for the work whereunto I have called them. And when they had fasted and prayed, and LAID THEIR HANDS ON THEM, they sent them away. So they, being sent forth by the Holy Ghost, departed unto Seleucia; and from thence they sailed to Cyprus.

The First Century Church was a worshipping church, a fasting church, and a praying church. They recognized the call upon Saul and Barnabas to go into a certain missionary work. So, they recognized and ordained them by the laying on of hands.

This exercise does two things:

- It supernaturally imparts wisdom and special abilities to perform the task
- It shows the people that the church leadership recognizes and approves these men.

I am an ordained Assemblies of God minister. At my ordination ceremony, what do you suppose was done? The laying on of hands. The sectional presbyters, executive presbyters, and general presbyters, all laid their hands on me and ordained me into the Gospel Ministry.

This is another purpose for the laying on of hands.

Authority is imparted or transmitted through the laying on of hands.

Next we'll learn how God often imparts healing through the laying on of hands.

CHAPTER

BESTOWING THE HEALING POWER OF GOD

We've taken a look at two objectives for the laying on of hands: First, to impart blessings; benefits; advantages. Secondly, to impart authority, as in ordaining ministers for service to the Church

Let's now look at a third purpose for the laying on of hands.

TO BESTOW THE HEALING POWER OF GOD

In the Great Commission, Jesus said,

> **Mark 16:17-18**
> And these signs shall follow them that believe...
> they shall LAY HANDS ON THE SICK, and
> they shall recover.

If you are a person who believes in the healing power of Christ, and have faith that God will use you in this capacity, you may go to a hurting, sick person and lay hands on him and fully expect him to be healed.

This promise is given in connection with the Great Commission to "Go ye into all the world and preach the gospel..." (Mark 16:15). Therefore, as a faith-filled Christian, if you find a sick unbeliever, perhaps in your neighborhood, you are authorized by the Lord to ask them if they would like you to lay hands on them. If they respond positively, you may then lay hands on them and "they shall recover." Then, you can lead them and their families to Christ. Paul used this method of ministering.

Acts 28:8-9
And it came to pass, that the father of Publius lay sick of a fever and of a bloody flux: to whom Paul entered in, and prayed, and LAID HIS HANDS ON HIM, and healed him. So when this was done, others also, which had diseases in the island came, and were healed.

Acts 19:11
And God wrought special miracles BY THE HANDS of Paul.

The other apostles practiced the laying on of hands in ministering to people.

Acts 5:12
And BY THE HANDS of the apostles wee many signs and wonders wrought among the people; and they were all with one accord in Solomon's porch.

It only makes sense to use the method that Jesus used so often. Of course, it's not the only method of transmitting God's healing power, but it is an effective method. Look at the ministry of Jesus:

Mark 5:22-23

And, behold, there cometh one of the rulers of the synagogue, Jairus by name; and when he saw him, he fell at his feet, and besought him greatly saying, My little daughter lieth at the point of death: I pray thee, come and LAY THY HANDS ON HER, that she may be healed; and she shall live.

Mark 6:5-6

And when the Sabbath day was come, he began to teach in the synagogue; and many hearing him were astonished, saying, From whence hath this man these things? And what wisdom is this which is given unto him, that even such mighty works are wrought BY HIS HANDS?

Mark 8:22-25

And he cometh to Bethsaida; and they bring a blind man unto him, and besought him to touch him. And he took the blind man by the hand, and led him out of the town; and when he had spit on his eyes, and PUT HIS HANDS UPON HIM, he asked him if he saw ought. And he looked up, and said, I see men as trees, walking. After that he PUT HIS HANDS AGAIN UPON HIS EYES, and made him look up: and he was restored, and saw every man clearly.

Luke 4:40

Now when the sun was setting, all they that had any sick with divers diseases brought them unto him; and he LAID HIS HANDS ON EVERY ON OF THEM, and healed them.

What is there about the laying on of hands that seems to bring the healing power of God into a situation?

I believe it first of all provides a deadline, or point of contact for the recipient to release their faith to God. In other words, they believe, "at the moment hands are laid upon me, I will receive my healing."

This is what the woman with the issue of blood did. She had been sick for several years, but finally set a deadline for her healing when she heard about Jesus, She said, "If I may touch but His clothes, I shall be whole." She set a deadline, a point at which she could release her faith for healing, and it worked!

> **Mark 5:29**
> And straightway the fountain of her blood was dried up; and she felt in her body that she was healed of that plague.

> **Mark 5:34**
> And he said unto her, Daughter, thy faith hath made thee whole: go in peace, and be whole of thy plague.

The laying on of hands provides a releasing point for faith. Secondly, it seems that actual power is bestowed by an anointed touch. When the woman touched Jesus, "immediately (He knew) in Himself that virtue (power) had gone out of him." (Mark 5:30).

Power went out of Jesus and into the woman when she touched Him.

Though this power cannot be seen in the natural, we can see the results of it. And when one who believes (Mark 16:17), and exercises faith (Heb. 11:1;6;21, Acts 3:16), lays hands on someone who is sick, it's sort of like a completed circuit and POWER FLOWS!

St. Paul was healed through the laying on of hands. He was blind, and God sent Ananias, a layman, to him to lay hands upon him. Look what happened:

Acts 9:17-18
And Ananias went his way, and entered into the house; and PUTTING HIS HANDS ON HIM said, Brother Saul, the Lord, even Jesus, that appeared unto thee in the way as thou camest , hath sent me, that thou mightest receive thy sight, and be filled with the Holy Ghost. And immediately there fell from his eyes as it had been scales: and he received sight forthwith, and arose, and was baptized.

Paul gives us more light on the incident in Acts.

Acts 22:12-16
And one Ananias, a devout man according to the law, having a good report of all the Jews which dwelt there, came unto me and stood, and said unto me, Brother Saul, receive thy sight. And the same hour I looked up upon him. And he said, The God of our fathers hath chosen thee, that thou shouldest know his will, and see that Just shouldest know his will, and see that Just One, and shouldest hear the voice of his mouth. For thou shalt be his witness unto all men of what thou hast seen and heard. And now why tarriest thou? Arise, and be baptized, and wash away thy sins, calling on the name of the Lord.

Three things happened when hands were laid on Paul:

1. He was healed completely; his sight was restored.
2. He received the baptism in the Holy Spirit.

3. He was given confirmation (probably through prophecy) of his calling and mission in life.

Healing is certainly offered through Christ's love and atonement. The laying on of hands is a means of helping people receive the healing power of God into their lives.

Every believer should receive "the power from on high." Someone said "the Baptism in the Holy Spirit is the mightiest power in the universe. " The laying on of hands helps you receive this encounter as we shall see next!

CHAPTER 5

HELPING BELIEVERS RECEIVE THE BAPTISM IN THE HOLY SPIRIT

We already mentioned how Paul received the baptism in the Holy Spirit through the laying on of hands. There were others also who received this glorious experience in this fashion. In fact, Paul himself ministered in this manner when praying for believers to receive.

Acts 19:6
And when Paul had LAID HIS HANDS UPON THEM, the Holy Ghost came on them; and they spoke with tongues, and prophesied.

Also, prior to Paul's conversion, a young evangelist named Philip was conducting revival services down in Samaria. There were signs and miracles, and great joy flooded that revival-filled city. But something was still missing. Let's look:

Acts 8:14-17
Now when the apostles which were at Jerusalem heard that Samaria had received the word of

> God, they sent unto them Peter and John: Who,
> when they were come down, prayed for the, that
> they might receive the Holy Ghost: (For as yet
> he was fallen upon none of them; only they were
> baptized in the name of the Lord Jesus) Then
> **LAID THEY THEIR HANDS ON THEM**, and
> they received the Holy Ghost.

In sixty percent of the Bible accounts of people receiving the baptism in the Holy Spirit, it was accomplished through the method of the laying on of hands! Again, it provides a releasing point for faith to go toward God to receive this promised experience.

When I pray for people to receive the baptism in the Holy Spirit, I prefer that others do not touch the person. You see, having several people lay hands on the person destroys the releasing point of faith. So, I merely tell the person, "When my hand touches your head, begin at that instant to worship in an unknown language. Cease praying and praising in English at that precise moment, and receive your heavenly prayer language."[6]

I have found that when people know what to do and when to do it, the miracle happens. Just recently in our Sunday services, I laid my hands on several people to receive the baptism in the Holy Spirit. The first person immediately began praising the Lord in another language. One, two, three, four, five, six, seven...one after the other, as I laid my hands on them, began to speak in heavenly languages they had never before learned.

One person said, "I can't even speak in English, and you expect me to speak in tongues?" But when I touched

---

6   See my book *Filled!*

her head with my hands, she immediately began speaking praises unto God in the beautiful language of the Spirit.

The laying on of hands can help believers receive this promise of power, the baptism in the Holy Spirit. Let's continue now and examine still another purpose in the laying on of hands.

I encourage you to get my book, *Filled!* for an in depth look at the Baptism in the Holy Spirit.

Next we will see how spiritual gifts can be released through the laying on of hands.

CHAPTER

TO REVEAL OR CONFIRM SOME SPIRITUAL GIFT

We've discussed four reasons for the practice of laying on of hands:

1. To impart blessings
2. To impart authority
3. To transmit the healing power of God
4. To help believers receive the baptism in the Holy Spirit

Now, we'll discuss a fifth Biblical reason for the laying on of hands.

This fifth reason is somewhat frightening to many Christians. I understand their apprehension. Years ago, a splinter Pentecostal group was formed with an unhealthy emphasis on imparting gifts through the laying on of hands. They were imparting gifts of "fixing buses." Gifts of "changing diapers." Along with other similar "gifts." I recognize that indeed people may be gifted in these and other areas, but this particular group became precariously extreme. The group has, over time, thankfully, come back to a scriptural approach to the laying on of hands.

But, along the way, most churches back lashed and withdrew so far from any of this "fanaticism," they began to completely ignore or reject the practice of the laying on of hands to reveal or confirm spiritual gifts. Nonetheless, it is a legitimate practice when properly administered.

Paul longed to see (in person) the church at Rome that he could come to impart some spiritual gift to each member.

> **Romans 1:11**
> For I long to see you, that I may impart unto you some spiritual gift, to the end ye may be established.

Paul likely had in mind the ministry of laying on of hands when he wrote this since other Scriptures give evidence of Paul's mode of imparting or confirming spiritual gifts.

> **II Timothy 1:6**
> Wherefore I put thee in remembrance that thou stir up the gift of God, which is in thee by the PUTTING ON OF MY HANDS.

> **I Timothy 4:14**
> Neglect not the gift that is in thee, which was given thee by prophecy, with THE LAYING ON OF HANDS Of the presbytery.

Apparently, it was quite proper and common for a prophecy to go forth over an individual upon whom hands were laid.

But let me make a remark at this point. It was normally the official church leaders who prophesied, not just any believer.

Caution and discretion must be exercised in this matter. I know of cases where individuals have received personal "prophecies" through some unauthorized "maverick," laying claim to apostolic authority, and have followed those "prophecies" to their bankruptcy and utter disappointment. Make sure the person who lays hands on you is a sensible, Spirit-directed, intelligent man or woman of God. What a great blessing when this ministry operates in purity and authenticity.

A PERSONAL EXPERIENCE

My wife and I had been in full-time ministry for only six months when things seemed to come to a grinding halt. We were teaching every week, I was on the radio in five states, and things seemed to moving forward rapidly. But suddenly, our finances dropped off for no apparent reason. We decided to take a trip to Texas to get away for a couple of weeks.

While there, we attended a large service where a fairly well-known preacher was ministering. At the close of the service we went up onto the stage and, he laid one hand on Mary Jo and one hand on me and began to prophesy. He told us exactly what we were going through, the solution, and what the future held for us and for our ministry. It has all come to pass, just as was revealed while he ministered through the laying on of hands.

There is something about the touching that God uses to supernaturally reveal things at times.

While in Detroit several years ago, we met a clean, but crudely dressed young man at a Gospel crusade. He seemed to be an intelligent young fellow, but appeared very poor. He was about 17 years old, I suppose. We asked how he was getting home and he told us he was walking.

We offered to give him a ride home. He was humbly reluctant at first but finally consented.

We drove through some of the roughest sections of the city, turned left, at his direction, onto a narrow, dark, street and pulled up to a dingy, old apartment building. Prior to arriving there, the Lord had already spoken to my heart about giving the guy some money, so I had discreetly pulled a twenty-dollar bill from my wallet. As he went to step from my car, I slapped the bill into his palm and suddenly, unexpectedly, like a flash, I knew something that I could not have known unless the Spirit of God revealed it. As soon as I touched his hand, revelation came instantly! I knew something! I knew it was his mother's birthday and that this young man felt terrible because he had no money to buy her a gift.

So, when he realized I had given him some cash, he asked, "What is this for?"

"It's to buy your mother a birthday present." I answered.

"How did you know? He asked, with an astonished look on his baby face. "How did you know?"

I thought the kid was going to cry, he became so emotionally choked up.

The point I'm trying to make is this: revelation sometimes comes by the touching through the laying on of hands. So, it's quite possible that certain gifts and ministries could be revealed in this manner.

In one of our evening services, I asked every person with a definite call to the ministry to come forward. Almost a hundred people came forward. I called for the pastoral staff and the elders to lay hands on them. We did, and many, encouraging, comforting, edifying things were revealed by the Spirit of God. It was amazing!

I'm not afraid to practice something just because there have been abuses and excesses. We must be careful that we don't stretch to the opposite extreme of an "extreme."

And so, the laying on of hands is an effective, scriptural means of revealing or confirming some spiritual gift, or giving some sort of needed revelation.

In the next chapter, we'll take a quick look at some of the mistakes associated with the laying on of hands.

NOTE: Please see my book, *Gifts that Shape Your Life and Change Your World* for a deeper study on spiritual gifts.

7

ABUSES, MYTHS, AND MISTAKES

Whenever there is something genuinely of God, you can be certain that the enemy will seek to mess it up somehow. He counterfeits. That's one method. He causes confusion. That's another method. He gets people to lay an undue emphasis upon a particular practice. That's still another method. He tries to get people to abuse, that which is genuine, so that it loses its beauty and value in people's eyes. That's perhaps him most effective method in the Church abuses.

Let's go over some of the most common abuses and mistakes associated with this ministry of laying on of hands.

MYTH: "JUST ANY OLE' BODY CAN LAY HANDS ON OTHERS"

This is a common thought, especially among full-gospel people. And in a sense, it's true. Anybody can lay hands on people, but that doesn't mean it's scriptural, nor does it mean it will be effective. This is why God can't turn the power up in some believer's lives. Because they want to do certain things whether or not those things are proper or scriptural.

There is one instance in the Bible where all believers are authorized to minister with the laying on of hands. And that's in the context of the Great Commission (Mark 16:17-18). Any believer may lay his hands upon a sick person and in faith fully expect him to recover. This is to be used in evangelism, such as neighborhood evangelism.

Usually the ministry of laying on of hands, however, is exercised by official church leaders; the presbytery (which consists of pastors, elders, bishops; in other words, the official spiritual leaders of the church.)

In Samaria, there was a fabulous, supernatural revival going on, but nobody laid hands on each other. Peter and John, two of the official church leaders, came down to Samaria and performed the laying on of hands (Acts 8:5-17).

With the exception of laying hands on the sick, with respect to evangelism, it is most always the official church leaders or their authorized delegates who minister in the laying on of hands.

In the home, the husband/father is the "pastor" so-to-speak. He may lay hands on any sick family member and expect them to recover.

ABUSE: INDISCRIMINATE LAYING ON OF HANDS

Another common mistake in the laying on of hands is it's indiscriminate practice. The Bible exhorts us:

I Timothy 5:22
Lay hands suddenly (indiscriminately) on no man

I think sometimes at altar services we've been careless in the laying on of hands. We've ruined the releasing point of faith for people seeking help. Deacon Henry lays hands on Sister Jones. Then along comes Deacon Charlie, with the best intentions, and he too lays hands on Sister Jones, while Deacon Henry moves onto Brother Smith. Then Pastor Doe sees that an added touch is needed in Sister Smith's life so he puts his hands on her, prays, then moves on. Oh yes, about this time, Sister Papoofnick "feels led" to lay hands on Sister Smith and pray over her...so she does. And the scene goes on... and on...and on.

Poor Sister Smith. The laying on of hands profited her nothing, because of improper use.

MISTAKE: NOT SEEKING THE GUIDANCE OF THE HOLY SPIRIT

Another mistake we commonly make, is failing to seek the Lord's direction in who and when to exercise the laying on of hands.

I know a pastor who passed by a lady in the healing line three times without laying hands on her. Finally, she stopped him and asked. "Why aren't you praying for me?" He responded with a word of knowledge, "Because you haven't come here for prayer. You've come here to mock me and somehow to make a fool out of me. Now get out of her! And I do mean NOW!

She took off like a lightning bolt, because she knew he was absolutely correct.

You must seek God to show you the faith-filled person and pray for that one first. Then there will likely be a chain reaction. People will see the results and it will encourage them to believe God.

One night in a service I prayed for a whole line of people to receive the baptism in the Holy Spirit. I asked the Lord for whom I should pray first. He showed me through an inner perception who was most ready to release their faith. Instantly, as I laid hands on her she began to praise God in tongues. Then another, then another, then another, right down the line. It's important to supernaturally perceive who has faith ready for releasing, and pray for that one first.

> **Acts 14:8-10 NLT**
> [8] While they were at Lystra, Paul and Barnabas came upon a man with crippled feet. He had been that way from birth, so he had never walked. He was sitting
>
> [9] and listening as Paul preached. Looking straight at him, Paul realized he had faith to be healed.
>
> [10] So Paul called to him in a loud voice, "Stand up!" And the man jumped to his feet and started walking.

When Ananias laid hands on Saul of Tarsus (Paul), he was clearly directed by the Holy Spirit. Guidance of the Holy Spirit is crucial in this ministry of the laying on of hands.

ABUSE: LAYING ON OF HANDS IN ARROGANCE

I have seen some clergymen lay hands on people in such an attitude of arrogance it was spiritually nauseating. One preacher said, "I'm going to zap you with the Holy Ghost when I touch you." This is disrespectful, does not honor God, and diminishes the sacredness of this exercise.

This practice must be entered into with great humility and reverence, not with a bold, ostentatious display of pride and arrogance. Humble yourself before the Lord and He'll reward you openly.[7] Get haughty and boastful, and you might as well prepare to take a plunge. Prepare to be embarrassed in full measure! (James 4:6-10)

Yes, the laying on of hands must be ministered with great respect and humility before the Lord. After all, it is He who does the real work. We are just instruments of His love and grace.

CONCLUSION

What a magnificent blessing when we believe, practice, and receive from the laying on of hands. Because God cares about us, He's provided special benefits, wisdom and authority, healing, baptism in the Holy Spirit, and the confirmation of spiritual gifts through the ministry of the laying on of hands.

Have you ever had hands laid on you for a blessing? Have you ever come to God's Son, Jesus, for the blessing of a new start in life? You can.

---

7   James 4:10, 1 Peter 5:5-6

LAYING ON OF HANDS

He said, "Whosoever will come to Me, I will in no wise cast out..." (John 6:37).

Maybe you've never made a profession of Jesus Christ. The Holy Spirit is speaking to your heart today saying, "This is your day to be empowered with genuine faith. Come to Jesus Christ now and let Him give you total victory over the destroying disease of worry."

God loves you more than you can imagine. But sin keeps us from enjoying a relationship with God because He is holy. But Jesus, God's son suffered and died, then rose from the dead so we could be declared, "not guilty" before His judgment. The "not guilty" verdict is for everyone who comes to Jesus Christ.

Right now, Jesus is standing at your heart's door.[8] If you have never known the love of Jesus Christ, if you are afraid of the future and you don't want to face it alone, then let me lead you in a prayer.

Jesus is saying to you:

"Do it my way. Don't try to do your own thing. I died on the Cross so that you can be part of my family, part of my kingdom. Just believe! Come to me and I won't turn you away. You don't even have to understand it all, simply believe, and act upon my Word. Come to me now. You've tried things your own way and it's gotten you nowhere. Do it my way now and I'll forgive all your sins and take you to heaven one day. On top of all that, I'll give you a clean slate and a new start in life right now."

---

8 Revelation 3:20

Pray this prayer with me:

> "Dear Lord Jesus, Please forgive me of all my sins and all the times I have ignored you and your Word. I believe you died on the cross for me, and I confess that you were raised from the dead. You said if I would come to you, that you would in no wise turn me away. So, I come to you in humble faith, renouncing my old ways, and asking you to fill me with your nature, and your Spirit. Make me a true disciple, full of faith, and gaining victory in every area of my life. Take me to heaven when this life is over. Thank you, Jesus Christ. I am forgiven. I am saved. I have a home in heaven now, and a brand-new start in life! Amen!"

I'd love to hear from you if you prayed that prayer with me.

I'd be honored to give you a free download of my book, *The New Life...Start of Something Wonderful.* It's yours free at **DaveWilliams.com/NL.**

You may write to me:

Dave Williams
P O Box 80825
Lansing, MI 48908-0825

Please include your comments and prayer requests when you write. Your letter is important to me.

Our e-mail address is: info@DaveWilliams.com

ABOUT DAVE WILLIAMS

Dave Williams is a teacher, trainer, and author. He coaches church leaders, business leaders, and followers of Christ on how to live a pacesetting life. Dave developed *The Art of Pacesetting Leadership* course (now available online). His three-pronged approach is (1) spiritual, (2) attitudinal, and (3) practical. Dave served as pastor of Mount Hope Church in Lansing, Michigan, for more than thirty years. In that time, thousands of ministers were trained through the Mount Hope Bible Training Institute, Dave Williams' Church Planter's School, and Dave Williams' School for Pacesetting Church Leaders.

With the help of staff and partners, a 72-acre campus with worship center was established including Bible Training Institute, children's center, Global Prayer Center, Valley of Blessing, Gilead Healing Center, care facilities, event center, café, fitness center, world evangelism headquarters, Global Communications

Center, and a state-of-the-art office complex with nine buildings.

During Dave's tenure 43 new Mount Hope Churches were launched in the United States, over 300 in West Africa, South Africa, Zimbabwe, and 200 in Asia with a combined membership exceeding 100,000. During his thirty-some years as pastor, Mount Hope Church gave over $40,000,000 to world missions.

He also served as a national general presbyter for the Assemblies of God, assistant district superintendent, executive presbyter, regent for North Central Bible College (now North Central University), and as a national missions' board member.

Dave hosted The Pacesetter's Path telecast on ABC and CBS affiliates, TCT Satellite system, and Golden Eagle Network for nineteen years which has been seen worldwide.

He was awarded his doctorate from Canada School of Theological Studies.

Dave is the author of over 60 books that teach and inspire readers in Christian growth, financial success, health, healing, and many other areas of Christian living. *The New Life: The Start of Something Wonderful* has sold over 3.5 million copies and has been translated into eight languages.

Dave's articles and reviews have appeared in national magazines such as *Advance, Pentecostal Evangel, Charisma Magazine, Ministry Today, Lansing Magazine, Detroit Free Press, World News,* and others.

Today, Dave serves as ambassador and "bishop" for Mount Hope Churches, and leads Dave Williams Ministries, Strategic Global Mission (charitable scholarships and grants), and Club 52 (for business people, high achievers, and entrepreneurs).

THE CENTER FOR PACESETTING LEADERSHIP

We equip pacesetters in every area, ready and prepared to do something great in the Kingdom; no mediocrity. We'd love for you to attend one of our seminars or schools. Here are a few courses at The Center For Pacesetting Leadership:

- Seminar for Today's Prophets and Seers
- Club 52 "Millionaires with a Mission!" See how easy it is to move to "millionaire status" by using Spiritual, Attitudinal, and Practical Principles. (Wealthy Place Seminars)
- Faith Goals Seminars and Retreats
- Demolishing Strongholds in Your Life and Family
- Understanding the role of Angels and How to Activate Heaven's Messengers
- The Art of Pacesetting Leadership
- Learning how to Flow in Supernatural Gifts of the Holy Spirit.

FAITH BUILDING PRODUCTS

THE OVERCOMING POWER OF FAVOR
(MP3 INSTANT DOWNLOAD)

Become one of God's "Favorites"!

How would you like to make a quantum leap into the realm of unstoppable miracles? Do you ever wonder why some people seem to have obvious favor from the Lord and others seem to be just "unlucky" in life?

If you are a blood-bought believer in Jesus, God's will is for you to live a blessed life, but sometimes you don't know how to receive his blessings. God is waiting to flood your life with his favor; you just need to discover how to open the floodgates!

God's favor brings you protection, increase, blessings, productivity, reward, preservation, protection, health blessings and more! One day in God's favor can reverse a lifetime of so called bad breaks and bad luck.

Turn Bad Breaks into Blessings and Become One of His "Favorites"

THE POWER OF PROPHETIC REVELATION
(MP3 INSTANT DOWNLOAD)

How One Prophetic Word from God can Propel You Into an Amazing Future!

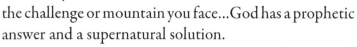

Whatever your uncertainty, whatever your doubt, whatever the challenge or mountain you face...God has a prophetic answer and a supernatural solution.

Right now, a connection exists between heaven and earth. God-made plans and secrets are ready to come from heaven. A deposit of God's glory for your life is available to you.

Do you believe God knows where the best jobs and investments are now?

A prophetic word can bring new levels of anointing, influence, and authority to your life and career and an extraordinary future!

Dr. Dave Williams shows you how to engage the prophetic realm and launch fresh miracles into your life, ministry, and business.

FILLED
(MP3 INSTANT DOWNLOAD)

If you believe Jesus is your Savior, you have access to the mightiest power in the universe. You can share in God's overflowing joy and peace; you can access God's power and presence in a very personal and intimate way. You can be filled with God's Holy Spirit.

Get ready for an experience that will change your spiritual life forever!

In this CD, Dr. Dave Williams leads you into an understanding of how to have a relationship and be filled with the Holy Spirit. He reveals:

- False beliefs people hold concerning the Holy Spirit
- The three dimensions of your relationship to the Holy Spirit
- The benefits of a relationship with the Holy Spirit
- How you can be filled with the Holy Spirit

SUPERNATURAL GIFTS OF THE HOLY SPIRIT
(MP3 INSTANT DOWNLOAD)

A Crash Course in Personality and Charismatic Gifts of the Holy Spirit

Do you need a solution? Are you tired of sitting on the sidelines of life? God has not left you alone; he sent you his Holy Spirit to come along side and help you. God has imparted in each of us, Kingdom Gifts of the Holy Spirit.

This powerful four-part series is the play book to discovering, developing, and deploying your gifts. In these lessons Dr. Dave coaches you on the biblical truths of seven personality gifts and nine gifts.

As you listen, you will discover the benefits of identifying your gifts and learn how to honor God's supernatural power in your life.

- Message 1: Personality Gifts
- Message 2: Charismatic Gifts: Part 1
- Message 3: Charismatic Gifts: Part 2
- Message 4: Charismatic Gifts: Part 3

YOGA CRAZE IN THE LAST DAYS
(AMAZON & KINDLE)

Jesus warned us of a coming Day in which deception would run rampant in the world. He warned that this Age of Deception would usher in a period known as "The Great Tribulation," where the world would be drawn into worshipping a false Messiah known as the Anti-christ. St. Paul said many would come under a strong delusion in the last days.

Yoga Craze in the Last Days will walk you through the truth about this ancient practice called "Yoga" and why so many are running to Yoga studios today. What is the weird appeal of Yoga? You'll discover the truth as you read this well- researched book.

24 REASONS TO AVOID YOGA: IF YOU ARE A CHRISTIAN
(AMAZON & KINDLE)

For those who want to warn others about Yoga in a succinct manner, we've produced a book with excerpts and commentary on the comprehensive book, *Yoga Craze in the Last Days.* Dr. Dave Williams takes you on a journey he never wanted to take—a journey into the world of deception and delusion. Most Christians have no idea what Yoga really is, and what it can do to their lives and family.

DAVEWILLIAMS.COM/YOGA

THE ART OF PACESETTING LEADERSHIP
(BOOK, DVD COURSE, ONLINE COURSE)

Keys to Gaining The Leading Advantage

Dave Williams is recognized as one of America's foremost authorities on leadership. In this course, you will learn the proven principles of leadership that will launch your life, ministry, business, or job to higher levels of success. Join him on a journey of discovery as he shares the secrets of developing the heart of an authentic leader.

Embark on one of the greatest endeavors of your life—becoming a pacesetting leader in whatever you are called to do. The principles in this course will advance your life, to greater levels of achievement as you begin to experience and practice the art of pacesetting leadership. These principles have transformed lives, businesses, and ministries for several decades—and they will transform your life and your calling as you put them into action.

DAVEWILLIAMS.COM/PL

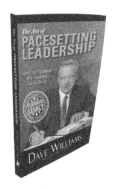

The Art of Pacesetting Leadership (Book)

- 37 Power packed chapters
- 313 pages of step-by-step pacesetting principles

ONLINE Course

- 16 Video Sessions
- Student Workbook Download
- The Art of Pacesetting Leadership Ebook
- MP3 Session Downloads
- Devotional Reflections

Leadership Course

- 16 sessions on DVD
- 16 audio recordings
- Hardcover book
- Student manual
- Moderator's manual
- License for unlimited public viewing

DAVEWILLIAMS.COM/PL

Made in the USA
Monee, IL
28 April 2023

32521636R00036